So You Think You Know?
MILTON KEYNES
A QUIZ & MISCELLANY

THE FRANCIS FRITH COLLECTION

D0506391

First published in the United Kingdom in 2005 by The Francis Frith Collection®

Hardback edition published in 2005 ISBN 1-84589-243-7

Text and Design copyright The Francis Frith Collection®
Photographs copyright The Francis Frith Collection® except where indicated.

British Library Cataloguing in Publication Data

So You Think You Know? Milton Keynes
Text adapted from original material supplied by Marion Hill

The Francis Frith Collection
Frith's Barn, Teffont,
Salisbury, Wiltshire SP3 5QP
Tel: +44 (0) 1722 716 376
Email: info@francisfrith.co.uk
www.francisfrith.co.uk

Printed and bound in England

Front Cover: **MILTON KEYNES, BALLOON RELEASE AT THE BOWL 1988** ZZZ05145t

The colour-tinting is for illustrative purposes only, and is not intended to be historically accurate

Modern photographs by Marion Hill unless otherwise specified.

Aerial photographs reproduced under licence from Simmons Aerofilms Limited.

The author and publisher gratefully acknowledge the assistance of Living Archive, Milton Keynes, in providing additional illustrative material for use in htis book.

Every attempt has been made to contact copyright holders of illustrative material.
We will be happy to give full acknowledgement in future editions for any items not credited.
Any information should be directed to The Francis Frith Collection.

AS WITH ANY HISTORICAL DATABASE, THE FRANCIS FRITH ARCHIVE IS CONSTANTLY BEING CORRECTED AND IMPROVED, AND THE PUBLISHERS WOULD WELCOME INFORMATION ON OMISSIONS OR INACCURACIES

CONTENTS

MILTON KEYNES MISCELLANY

The 150-million-year old fossilised remains of an Icthyosaurus (Fish Lizard) were discovered in an excavation bucket when workers were digging foundations for the city's Caldecotte Lake in 1972.

The first known lost property in the city area was left in Loughton, Pennyland and Fenny Stratford 10,000 years ago - by Stone Age people dropping their flint weapons.

The city's tributary of the River Great Ouse, the River Ouzel (which enters the city at Water Eaton, passes Roman Fenny Stratford, medieval Caldecotte, and the Domesday villages of Simpson, Walton, the Woolstones, Milton Keynes Village and Willen) - is also known as the River Lovat.

Iron Age people - who used iron tools and weapons - are known to have lived in farming communities around 3,000 years ago in Fenny Stratford, Westcroft, Downs Barn, Pennyland, Woughton and Blue Bridge.

A 1,000-year-old grave discovered at Tattenhoe contained the body of a still-born baby: three animal bones had been laid over its lower half, giving rise to theories that it was either the secret burial of an illegitimate or deformed child, or the ritual dedication of a new building.

The Roman-built Watling Street (the original A5), a vital artery from London to Chester for 2,000 years, was built eight metres wide and elevated in towns - hence the 'High' Streets of Stony and Fenny Stratford.

Queen Boudicca (or Boadicea) of the Essex Iceni tribe was defeated by the Romans in an ambush just north of Milton Keynes; a terrible blizzard of javelins slaughtered 80,000 of her warriors.

The Bancroft Roman villa was just one of eight large farming estates created 2,000 years ago in the city area, each centred on a Roman villa. The others were in Milton Keynes Village, Stantonbury, Wymbush, Walton, Dovecote Farm at Shenley Brook End, Bletchley's Sherwood Drive and Holne Chase.

The Domesday Book of 1086 records eighteen city area communities which were then the villages of Bradwell, Broughton, Caldecotte (near modern Tongwell), Calverton, Great Linford, Loughton, Milton Keynes Village, Shenley Brook End, Shenley Church End, Simpson, Stantonbury, Water Eaton, Wavendon, Westbury, Wolverton, Little Woolstone, Great Woolstone and Woughton.

A pilgrim's bottle (for holy water) was left behind in the 14th-century chapel at Bradwell Abbey, and so was a pin-up badge for St Thomas à Becket, the 12th-century archbishop who was murdered in Canterbury Cathedral.

MILTON KEYNES, OLD BRADWELL'S BEER AND BUN RACE c1983 ZZZ05143
(Reproduced by courtesy of Living Archive)

In 1250, travellers were able to make their way from Newport Pagnell to Loughton on a new road called The Portway (also the name of the city's modern H5 grid road into Central Milton Keynes).

Milton Keynes has over 20 Scheduled Ancient Monuments, including six homesteads with moats and medieval fishponds (Milton Keynes Village, the Shenleys, the Woolstones and Loughton); three deserted medieval villages (Great Linford, Caldecotte and Woughton); and three motte and bailey castles (Old Wolverton, Shenley Church End, and Bradwell).

The oldest domestic building in the city is a 700-year-old house in Broughton Road, Milton Keynes Village, a timber-framed thatched house complete with its original roof timbers and base cruck - massive curved beams stretching from the ground to the eaves. The manor was acquired by Phillip Aylesbury c1302 when he married Margaret de Kaynes. The house was probably built c1320 and inhabited by his bailiff. The Bird family of carpenters lived there for six generations from 1789 (see page 46).

The phrase 'a cock and bull story' is thought to have originated from the fanciful tales told by travellers as they went from one 15th-century Stony Stratford hostelry (the Cock Inn) to another (the Bull Inn nearby).

BLETCHLEY, TREE SQUARE c1955 B439017

20 people were turned out of their cottages in 1506 when the monks of Bradwell Priory enclosed 300 acres in order to keep a more lucrative 'crop' of sheep. 30 years later in 1536, when King Henry VIII dissolved the monasteries to access their wealth, the monks themselves were turned out.

Wolverton has the earliest parish registers of the city area, dating from 1535.

The Gunpowder Plot of 1605 was hatched at Sir Everard Digby's manor house in Gayhurst, five miles from Milton Keynes.

Walton Hall Manor House was once home to the Harley family of Harley Street, and has been home to the Open University since 1969.

Many city places recall ancient field names in the area: Connie Burrough Hill and Long Neath Hill (1641); Brinklow Hill (1680); The Downes (1690); Greenleys, Hodge Furze and Fullers Slade (1742); Great Holme and Childs Way (1769); Groveway, Netherfield and Ashland (1781); Rooksley (1790); and Blakelands (1860).

MILTON KEYNES
THE WILLEN PEACE PAGODA
1980 ZZZ05132 (Reproduced by courtesy of Living Archive)

MILTON KEYNES, A REMNANT OF WARTIME IN 1987 ZZZ05140
(Reproduced by courtesy of Living Archive)

In the 17th and 18th centuries around 30 'service stations' - alehouses and their stables - traded alongside or near Watling Street in the Milton Keynes area.

In 1737, Dick Turpin, the famous highwayman, was said to have visited the Old Swan at Woughton, and reversed his horse Black Bess's shoes so that his pursuers would set off after him in the wrong direction.

Among the centuries-old coaching inns which still trade today in the city are Stony Stratford's Old George, White Horse and Crown pubs, Fenny Stratford's Bull & Butcher and Swan pubs, the Nag's Head in Great Linford, the Old Swan Inns of both Milton Keynes Village and Woughton, and the Fountain at Loughton.

The 70-odd Stony Stratford occupations of the 1790s included sixteen victuallers, fifteen grocers, nine carpenters and eight bakers, as well as a collar-maker, a fisherman and net-maker, a hemp-dresser and roper, an alesman, a staymaker, a surveyor of houses and windows, a potash-maker, a toyman and a tinman.

Wolverton Station's famous Refreshment Room (1858-1881) was staffed by seven waitresses, four men, three boys, a cook, his kitchen-maid, two scullery-maids, two housemaids, two laundry-maids, one baker, one baker's boy, one garden-boy, an 'odd man', and a superintendent matron. Annually they served 182,500 Banbury cakes, 56,940 queen cakes, 29,200 pâtés, 43,800lbs meat (including pork pies made from the company's 85 pigs), 16,425 quarts of milk, 25,692 bottles of ale, 2,392 bottles of brandy, and 666 bottles of gin.

In 1860, McConnell's Bloomer engine No 372 was involved in a race against time to avert war between America and Britain. Carrying the 'Trent Dispatches', which had to be received by the British Government within five hours, the Bloomer averaged 65 mph - despite fog - and arrived with three minutes to spare.

Wolverton Works was an internationally renowned leader in industrial development: in 1901, the Works' Power House was the first in the UK to be completely lit and powered electrically; in 1903 the Cape Colony joined the queue in acquiring Wolverton-trained railway fitters, coach-body makers, and track maintenance men to work on the new South African Railway; and demands for the Works' engineers came from all over the world, including Australia, Asia and the Americas.

STONY STRATFORD, HIGH STREET 1906 S266001

MILTON KEYNES, THE M1 AT JUNCTION 14 c1965 M388050

People settled in the new towns of Wolverton and New Bradwell in the 19th century from all over the country: their birth-places ranged from London to Scotland, Birmingham, Lancashire, Cornwall, Cumberland, Wales and Essex.

Wolverton Works created specialised carriages for milk vans, vans for sausages (17 tons) and bananas (10 tons); sealed vans for gunpowder or bullion (with special locks and steel-plated floors); customised trucks for beer-tanks, farm equipment, and sheet plate glass; a 'bogie-bolster wagon' to carry 50 tons of rails; travelling post offices; saloons for diners, sleepers and invalids; 'Club Saloons' for businessmen, a 'Saloon de Luxe' with brass bedsteads and Wilton pile carpets; and the Royal Train.

The combined population of Wolverton and New Bradwell in 1901 was 9,200
- larger than either Aylesbury or Buckingham. In all Buckinghamshire, only
High Wycombe was larger.

WOLVERTON, STRATFORD ROAD c1910 W176501

MILTON KEYNES, THE SHOPPING BUILDING, INTERIOR 2005 M388718k

In 1900-1902, George Cave's Solid Beer Syndicate in Bletchley supplied Boer War troops with dried blocks of beer.

By 1906 5,000 workers were employed on the 80-acre Wolverton Works site.

Hayes Boatyard, Watling Works in Stony Stratford closed in 1925 having spent 65 years building boats for, among others, Britain, France, Russia and Egypt. Built in 1924, the 'Wey', the last of 300 vessels built at the yard, is now on show at Milton Keynes Museum at Stacy Hill.

In the Second World War, in addition to its civilian work, Wolverton Works repaired Whitley, Wellington and Stirling bomber aircraft; supplied radar cabins for the Battle of Britain; produced submarine-detecting devices, and gunsights for the American Lewis gun; built Horsa gliders, gun-carriages, and limbers; forged 166,910 shells and 432,819 shell-containers for chemical bombs; and constructed 8,442 assault boats, 169 mobile cranes, and 37 lift trucks - as well as making aircraft-towing equipment, tree-hauling wagons, thousands of mine-detectors, and catamarans for the Navy.

Before the railway's huge demand saw brickworks proliferate throughout the city area in the 19th and early 20th centuries, Denbigh had Milton Keynes's earliest brickyard, Bailey's, in 1700; Woughton recorded John Eastment as a brick-maker in 1728, and Caldecotte's 1750s brickworks were excavated by city developers in the 1980s.

In the 1950s, the London Brick Company provided a hostel in Drayton Parslow for their workers, who came from several countries: Poland, the Ukraine, Yugoslavia, Czechoslovakia and Italy, including ex-prisoners of war.

In the 1970s, Bletchley Brickworks were making 4½ million bricks a week - over 230 million a year - and employed 375 men.

The Reverend W T Sankey, Vicar of St Giles in Stony Stratford (1859-1875), built New Street leading to the new vicarage, and demolished over 30 old slum dwellings and the ancient Horseshoe Inn to make way for a new infants' school with a parish hall.

'Britain's best-kept secret' of the Second World War, Bletchley Park, later housed a Teachers' Training College, the Diplomatic Wireless Service, the Ministry of Aviation, and British Telecom. It is now run by a trust dedicated to preserving its pioneering war-time importance in computerised code-breaking - which succeeded because of geniuses like the mathematician Alan Turing and the novelist Angus Wilson, and because of the anonymous thousands of 'geese who laid the golden egg and never cackled' (Winston Churchill).

When the M1 opened in 1959, three million vehicles were registered in the country: 14,000 used Milton Keynes's section of the M1 daily. (It was ten times that number 40 years later). There was no 70mph limit; top speeds of 150mph and averages of 80mph were routinely recorded.

MILTON KEYNES, THE STOCKS AT OLD BRADWELL c1900 ZZZ05103
(Reproduced by courtesy of Wolverton and District Archaeological Society)

BLETCHLEY PARK, THE MANSION c1960 B439072

Milton Keynes was the first place in the UK to be designated as a new city - not a new town (1967).

The shopping building - visited by Queen Elizabeth II and opened by the Prime Minister in1979 - attracted 250,000 people a week by its first Christmas; people came from Cheltenham, Birmingham, Cambridge, North London, even Carlisle in the north and the south coast. Now, around 30 million visitors a year (600,000 shoppers weekly) come to shop in the city; at Christmas, two million more customers have been recorded in Milton Keynes than visit the Trafford Centre in Manchester.

Milton Keynes was the first place in the world to accommodate a successful distance-learning university: the Open University began in 1969, and is based in Milton Keynes.

Milton Keynes was one of the locations for the film 'Superman IV'. Film stars Christopher Reed and Gene Hackman acted alongside hundreds of Milton Keynes citizens (the 'extras') at the first phase of the Central Business Exchange - CBX1 - in 1986.

MILTON KEYNES, THE AQUEDUCT OVER GRAFTON STREET (V6) 2005 M388708k

Milton Keynes was one of the first UK places to have cable television (55% of city households had cable television by 1988), with all new housing automatically linked to the system.

An old brick-pit was converted by the judicious use of spoil to form an amphitheatre, the National Bowl, a venue for 65,000 people to enjoy Soul in the Bowl (1979), Police (1981) Thin Lizzy (1982) and three days of David Bowie in 1983. In 1989, the Bowl hosted the two-day Virat Hindu Sammelan (Great Hindu Assembly) which attracted over 55,000 Hindus, the largest ever gathering outside India.

By 1992, when Milton Keynes Development Corporation was wound up, the city was the base for 2,900 businesses, of which 2,660 had been attracted to Milton Keynes and over 250 were from North America, Europe and Japan. An average of 150 companies had arrived each year; nearly £2½-billion had been invested; 2 million square metres of commercial premises had been developed, and 80,000 jobs had been created.

The service sector makes up 75% of the jobs in Milton Keynes, in retail, education and training, software and hardware design, banking, insurance and management consultancy. Amongst the manufacturing facilities is still - 167 years on - the oldest continuously functioning railway factory in Britain, possibly in the world: Alstom is based at the old Wolverton Works.

MILTON KEYNES, THE SHOPPING BUILDING 2005   M388717k

NEW BRADWELL, THE OLD WINDMILL c1955   N224164

Bletchley's 'Blue Lagoon' hosts sixteen of the city's seventeen species of dragonfly, including the Southern Hawker, the Common Darter and the Emperor.

Birds considered 'very rare' in Buckinghamshire have been sighted at Willen (red-throated diver), New Bradwell (black-throated diver), and Caldecotte (great northern diver). City birdwatchers have also recorded five species each of grebe and owl, eight of goose, nine of warbler, eleven of gull, and the honey buzzard, red kite and osprey among twelve birds of prey, along with escaped parrots, budgerigars, cockatoos, canaries - and even an albatross.

MILTON KEYNES, BALLOON RELEASE AT THE BOWL 1988 ZZZ05145
(Reproduced by courtesy of Living Archive)

In 1967 the target population of Milton Keynes was 250,000. This was revised downwards in 1992 to 200,000. By 2011, the total will have risen to 255,780 people; and the target is now 350,000. In 2031, Milton Keynes will be the twelfth largest urban area in the UK.

WOLVERTON, A STEAM TRAIN CROSSING THE VIADUCT c1900 ZZZ05116
(Living Archive Collection, courtesy of Baz Green)

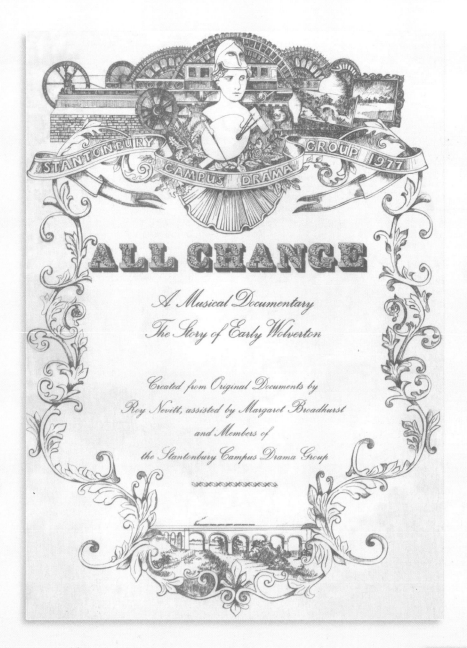

STANTONBURY CAMPUS DRAMA GROUP 1977

ALL CHANGE

A Musical Documentary

The Story of Early Wolverton

Created from Original Documents by
Roy Nevitt, assisted by Margaret Broadhurst
and Members of
the Stantonbury Campus Drama Group

STONY STRATFORD, JOHN WESLEY'S TREE, MARKET PLACE ZZZ05110
(Reproduced by courtesy of Living Archive)

MILTON KEYNES QUIZ QUESTIONS

1. What was the first known living creature in the Milton Keynes city area, and how long ago did it live here?

2. Where and when did people in the Milton Keynes area first settle?

3. What has been the most formidable and uncontrollable problem for people living in the city area until 30 years ago?

4. How long - from source to outlet - is the River Great Ouse, which skirts the city's northern edge?

5. What was discovered in the foundations of the County Arms in New Bradwell in the 1860s?

6. Who were Wulfere, Bleca, and Brede, and what did they leave behind?

7. What happened nearly 1,100 years ago behind Milton Keynes council offices?

8. When was the largest change of land ownership in the city area before Milton Keynes came?

9. Why is 1194 an important date for Stony Stratford, and 1204 equally important for Fenny Stratford?

10. What do Pennsylvania USA and Stony Stratford have in common?

GREAT LINFORD, BLACK HORSE BRIDGE c1965 G347070

11. Where in the city is the probable site of the ancient public gallows for hanging law-breakers?

12. What unwelcome visitor came to Stony Stratford in 1609, 1625 and 1647, and to Fenny Stratford in 1665, with devastating consequences?

13. What 350-year-old monument was deliberately destroyed in Stony Stratford High Street in 1646, and why?

14. What crucial development for trade arrived in the city area in 1658?

15. What is the link between Willen's Church of Mary Magdalen and Sir Christopher Wren?

STONY STRATFORD, THE PARISH CHURCH c1955 S266011

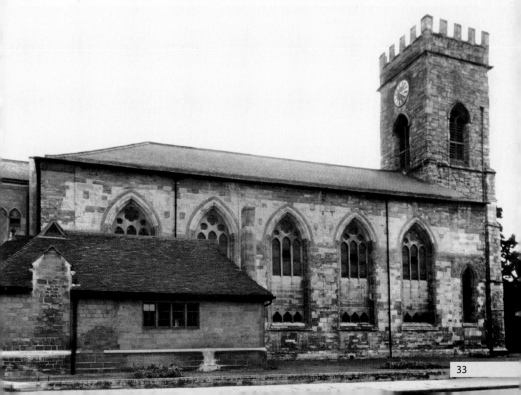

16. What, in Great Linford, cost £151 to build and remained in their original use for 280 years, until the 1960s?

17. Why were brass-pin factories and pillow-stand production so important to local trade in the 17th century?

18. Which rich benefactor financed, among other projects, the Church of St Martin in Fenny Stratford, though 'he was obliged towards the end of his days to dress meanly and to live in squalor, becoming very dirty and penurious so that he was often taken for a beggar'?

19. Which 74-year-old on a mission came to Stony Stratford in 1777?

20. What commercially significant meeting took place in the Bull in Stony Stratford in 1792?

MILTON KEYNES, THE CHURCH OF ST MARY MAGDALENE, WILLEN 2005 ZZZ05108
(Reproduced by courtesy of Nick Bland, The Parks Trust)

WOLVERTON, OUTSIDE THE WORKS c1910 ZZZ05160
(Living Archive Collection, courtesy of Baz Green)

21. What was designed in 1800, collapsed in 1809, rebuilt in 1816, refurbished in the 1920s and has remained steadfastly aloft ever since?

22. Where in the city is a disused canal which was built over by a railway, and later became a cycle and pedestrian way?

23. What famous son of a famous father built the bridges at Newcastle, and at Berwick, and over the Menai Straits in Wales, and over the St Lawrence River in Canada, and the viaduct at Wolverton?

24. What huge development has been considered 'a wonder of modern times'?

25. What 'perfection' did the Royal Family receive from Wolverton for nearly 150 years?

26. What outrageous bloomer did James McConnell make in 1851?

27. What were the 'Toot' and the 'Tute'?

MILTON KEYNES, THE FUTURE OF QUEENS COURT ZZZ05156
(Reproduced by courtesy of Milton Keynes Partnership)

BLETCHLEY, A THATCHED COTTAGE, CHURCH GREEN ROAD 2005 B439701k

28. How did Stony Stratford's High Street become essential to many a successful maiden voyage and become linked to a disastrous one?

29. How could Mr H Ackroyd Stuart have become famous throughout the world with people speaking his name daily, even today?

30. What secret was sold in 1939 and did not become known until the mid 1980s?

31. What newcomer arrived on Milton Keynes's doorstep in 1959 and looks like growing even bigger in the next few years?

WOLVERTON, THE GRAND UNION CANAL c1960 W176076

A MAP OF THE BLETCHLEY AREA 1599 ZZZ05107 (Reproduced by courtesy of Living Archive)

32. What do Dolby Sound, Radio One and breath-tests have in common?

33. What opened its doors in 1969 to a flood of hundreds of thousands?

34. What 'first' did the sun shine on in 1972?

35. What now prevents flooding - which plagued residents for centuries - in the built-up areas of the city?

36. When, where and what was the first in the west, commemorated with an elephant in attendance?

37. What was the point in 1985? What was so special about it?

38. What strings, beads and settings account for 20% of the whole?

39. What city-run competition inspired a national efficiency movement?

40. What Milton Keynes construction was the first water-carrier in England for 50 years?

41. Where and when did a Roman Catholic cardinal preach before a sovereign for the first time in 400 years?

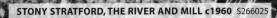
STONY STRATFORD, THE RIVER AND MILL c1960 S266025

MILTON KEYNES, THE OLDEST HOUSE, BROUGHTON ROAD 2005 M388706k

42. What finished after 25 years in the city in 1992?

43. What was finished in the city after 25 years in 1995?

44. What stood alone in the city after 1997?

45. All changed in 1999 - why?

STONY STRATFORD, THE WOLVERTON STEAM TRAM IN THE FLOOD ZZZ05098
(Reproduced by courtesy of Living Archive)

46. Why did Gilbert and George come to Milton Keynes in 1999?

WOLVERTON, THE CONGREGATIONAL CHURCH c1955 W176048

WOLVERTON, THE WORKS ZZZ05118 (Reproduced by courtesy of Living Archive)

47. What was the city area's population in 1967, and what had it grown to by 2004?

48. Apart from people, whose population has also dramatically increased since the start of the new city?

GREAT LINFORD, THE CHURCH FROM THE CANAL ZZZ05115
(Reproduced by courtesy of The Parks Trust)

49. What runs for 150 miles?

50. How young is Milton Keynes?

MILTON KEYNES, LEDA AND THE SWAN, WILLEN SOUTH ZZZ05151
(Reproduced by courtesy of Nick Bland, The Parks Trust)

MILTON KEYNES, THE TREE CATHEDRAL, CAMPBELL PARK, FROM THE AIR
ZZZ05147 (Reproduced by courtesy of Brian Wallis, The Parks Trust)

MILTON KEYNES QUIZ ANSWERS

1. The Icthyosaurus, or Fish Lizard, was excavated in the foundations of Caldecotte Lake in 1982, its fossilised bones estimated as being 150 million years old.

2. People first settled at Heelands in the Milton Keynes area, 4,500 years ago in around 2,500 BC.

3. Widespread flooding from the River Great Ouse and its tributaries the River Ouzel and Loughton Brook has devastated local communities in the past - until the city's storm-water balancing lakes controlled it.

4. The River Great Ouse is 140 miles long from its source near Silverstone in Northamptonshire to the Wash and the North Sea at King's Lynn.

5. A metalworker's hoard of bronze axes, spearheads and swords was found at the County Arms, New Bradwell, in the 1860s – the hoard was around 4,000 years old.

6. They left their names for city communities: their 'tun' (place), 'lea' (meadow) or 'well' was at Wolverton, Bletchley and Bradwell respectively.

7. In AD 914, residents of the Milton Keynes area had their first seat of local government on Seckloe Mound.

8. In 1066, William the Conqueror summarily confiscated land belonging to the defeated Anglo-Saxons and rewarded his Norman knights with 22,000 acres of the city area.

9. Stony Stratford was given its market charter in 1194 - only the second in the county; Fenny Stratford got its charter in 1204.

10. John Penn owned Stony Stratford mill in 1581. His descendants went on to found the state of Pennsylvania, USA.

11. Gallows are thought to have been on Watling Street (the old A5) just south of Stony Stratford, on the east side of the road, mid-way between Ridgeway (H1) and Millers Way (H2) at the end of Malvern Drive in Fullers Slade.

12. The Great Plague visited Stony Stratford in 1609 with 102 fatalities and again in 1625 killing 123; it returned in 1647 with 43 deaths, and devastated Fenny Stratford in 1665 with 129 casualties, closing down its market for years.

13. Stony Stratford's Eleanor Cross, one of several erected on the funeral route in 1296 by a grieving widower - King Edward I - was destroyed by anti-Royalists who supported Oliver Cromwell's Parliamentary army in the Civil War.

14. In 1658, the first London-Chester stage coach travelled along Watling Street through Fenny and Stony Stratford.

15. The eminent scientist and architect Robert Hook designed Willen's Church of St Mary Magdalene; he was a close colleague of Sir Christopher Wren.

16. The six one-roomed almshouses with outdoor toilets at Great Linford Manor were inhabited until the 1960s. They were refurbished as art and craft workshops in the 1980s.

17. The lace making industry, which was widespread throughout the city area, needed brass pins to hold the lace and pillows to rest it on.

18. Browne Willis (1682-1760), historian and antiquarian of Water Hall (the site of Bletchley Park) and then Whaddon Hall. He spent much of his fortune on churches in Bletchley, Stony Stratford and Fenny Stratford.

19. John Wesley preached in Stony Stratford's Market Square - under a tree, remnants of which still remain after over 200 years.

20. In June 1792, the plan for the new 90-mile Grand Junction Canal was discussed at the Bull, Stony Stratford between the proposer, the engineer John Barnes, and local worthies, including a major funder, the Marquis of Buckingham.

21. This is the aqueduct carrying the Grand Junction Canal across the River Great Ouse. The original wooden one collapsed; then in 1816 William Jessup built the Iron Trunk at Wolverton, still strong nearly 180 years later.

22. The Railway Walk from Bradwell to Great Linford was first a branch canal to Newport Pagnell (1817); then it was filled in for a branch railway between Wolverton and Newport (1865); when this closed in 1965, it was destined to become forgotten and overgrown - until the new city's Redways came along.

23. Robert Stephenson (1803-59) was the son of George Stephenson (1781-1848), the British engineer who invented the 'Rocket' - the world's first steam engine. Robert engineered the 112 miles of the London and Birmingham Railway, including all the bridges, embankments, cuttings and viaducts for the Milton Keynes area.

24. The historian Dr Lipscombe said this of the huge Wolverton Works in 1844.

25. The Royal Train was made at Wolverton from 1843 until 1975 - with, as the Wolverton Works Guide of 1906 said, 'decoration in the best possible taste, free from all gaudiness and exaggeration, the highest perfection attained in carriage building in England.'

26. In 1851, the prominent railway engineer James McConnell built the first of his 'masterpieces' at Wolverton - prototype express trains called 'Bloomers', so-called because their exposed wheelbase recalled the American Mrs Amelia Bloomer, whose daring designs showed her legs.

27. The Toot was the medieval lookout of a castle at Shenley, and the 'Tute' was the nickname for Wolverton's Science and Arts Institute, which operated from 1864 to 1970.

MILTON KEYNES QUIZ ANSWERS

28. Between 1860 and 1925, Hayes' tugboats were hauled from the boatyard on London Road up Stony's High Street by traction steam engine to the canal at Old Stratford, where they were launched. One of Hayes' apprentices was Sir Frederick Rebbeck KBE; he helped to design the 'Titanic' - which sank in 1912 on her maiden voyage.

29. Mr H Ackroyd Stuart of the ironworks in Denmark Street, Bletchley could have been more successful in promoting his patented product - an oil-fired engine - in 1890, seven years before Mr R Diesel built his. We could have been driving Ackroyd-Stuart cars!

30. Bletchley Park in modern Milton Keynes was sold to GCHQ in 1939. Its secret decoding role in the Second World War was not publicised until nearly 40 years later.

31. The M1 opened in 1959. Plans are currently afoot to increase it to four lanes in the Milton Keynes area.

32. They were all born in the same year that Milton Keynes was designated as a New City - 1967.

33. The Open University opened in Milton Keynes in September 1969, when the River Great Ouse flooded all around its headquarters at Walton Hall; by the 25th anniversary (in 1998) of its first graduation ceremony, 200,000 students had graduated.

34. The UK's first solar-heated house was built at Bradville, Milton Keynes.

35. To prevent the age-old problem of flooding in the city area, eleven balancing lakes were constructed from 1975 as storm-water storage reservoirs; they hold excess rainwater until the storm has abated and the city's swollen rivers (Great Ouse, Ouzel and Loughton Brook) have subsided. The lakes are automatically adjusted at the Cotton Valley Control Centre. They are Tongwell Lake, Brickkiln Reservoir, Bradwell Reservoir, Lodge Lake, Loughton Reservoir, Furzton Reservoir, Mount Farm Lake, Simpson Reservoir, Caldecotte Lake, Walton Lake, and Willen Lake.

36. The foundation ceremony of the west's first Peace Pagoda was at Willen in Milton Keynes in 1980 when a lengthy procession of Buddhist monks was headed by a richly draped elephant.

37. The Point multiplex cinema opened in the city centre in 1985 - the first in Britain - and heralded a huge national increase in cinema audiences.

38. The city's linear parks, managed by the independent Parks Trust, cover 4,500 of the city's 22,000 acres. The strings are tracks for walking, cycling and horse-riding; the beads are sports-centres, lakeside cafes and activity areas; and the settings are woods, paddocks, a golf course and a farm for handicapped children.

39. Energy World was a housing competition run by Milton Keynes Development Corporation in 1986 with 51 houses constructed at Knowlhill and Shenley Lodge to demonstrate energy efficiency. The unprecedented Milton Keynes Energy Cost Index inspired greater awareness of energy-efficient standards throughout the nation.

40. In 1991 a new £4-million aqueduct was built over the grid-road V6 Grafton Street for the Grand Union Canal. Four times as long as Wolverton's 170-year-old Iron Trunk (120m), it was the first to be built in the nation for half a century - with not only a towpath but, alongside it, the celebrated city-wide Milton Keynes Redway cycling system.

41. In March 1992, the dedication ceremony of the city centre church - Christ the Cornerstone - involved the leaders of the four main Christian churches of the UK, including the Roman Catholic Cardinal Basil Hume; his sermon in front of Queen Elizabeth II was the first before a reigning sovereign since the time of Queen Mary in the 1590s.

42. Milton Keynes Development Corporation was wound up in 1992 having been specifically tasked with building the new city.

43. The 50,000th new house for the city since 1970 was completed in 1995.

44. Milton Keynes Council became a Unitary Authority in 1997 - it was no longer part of Buckinghamshire County Council.

45. The Milton Keynes Theatre opened. The first dramatic production staged there in its preliminary 'community' week was the musical documentary drama 'All Change', the story of the railway coming to Wolverton in the 19th century, produced by the Living Archive.

46. Milton Keynes Gallery opened with an exhibition by the acclaimed international artists Gilbert and George.

47. The city area's population in 1967 was 40,000. In 2004, it was 180,000, and the population of Milton Keynes Borough as a whole was 240,000 (Milton Keynes Council population figures, 2004).

48. Wildlife has dramatically increased since the city was born - particularly birds and wild flowers, according to the Milton Keynes Natural History Society (see their book 'More Than Concrete Cows').

49. The Redways - the city's cycling and pedestrian routes - cover 230 kilometres (150 miles) around Milton Keynes city.

50. The average age of Milton Keynes citizens is 36 years of age compared with the rest of England at 40 years; around 25% of the MK population is under 18 years (MKC population figures 2004).

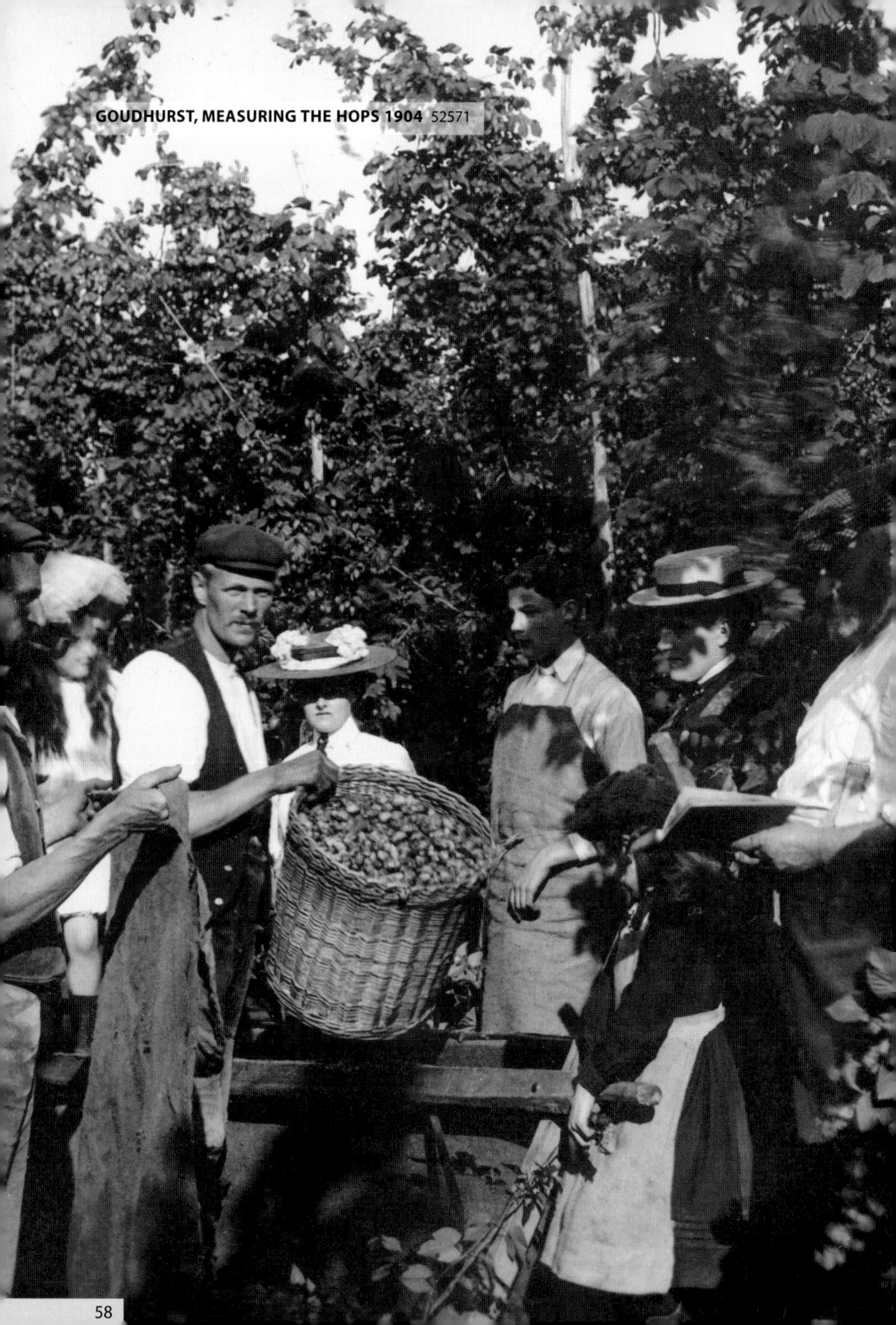

GOUDHURST, MEASURING THE HOPS 1904 52571

GENERAL HISTORY QUIZ QUESTIONS

1. Which 20th-century Prime Minister was a proficient bricklayer and a member of the union?

2. In Victorian times, what powerful substance did many fashionable society ladies use to spice up their afternoon tea parties?

3. What was the first battle of the English Civil War on 23 October 1642?

4. Who was Queen Victoria's first Prime Minister?

5. Which Michigan-born dentist was arrested in Canada for the murder of his wife in London?

6. For what crime was Titus Oates pilloried in the stocks and flogged every year?

7. What crime was committed by Burke and Hare?

8. What language was Elizabeth I not fluent in? German, French, Latin, or Italian?

9. In 1834 six Dorset farm labourers were transported to Australia. By what name are these men usually known?

HORNING, ON THE BROADS 1902 48108

MARKET DRAYTON, MARKET DAY 1911 63338

10. At which battle was Richard III slain?

11. Who was the first Prime Minister to live at Chequers?

12. Who was the leader of the Women's Social and Political Union?

13. In which year were women granted the vote on the Isle of Man? 1881, 1902, 1912, or 1946?

RHYL, DONKEYS ON THE SANDS 1891 29151

14. Which king signed the Magna Carta in 1215 at Runnymede?

15. In which city was the infamous Peterloo Massacre on 16 August 1819?

16. Who were the mother and father of Elizabeth I?

17. Before the French Revolution in 1789, who is reported to have said 'Let them eat cake'?

18. Who wore two shirts in which to be executed, and why?

19. Which queen was known as Bloody Mary?

20. Who was the only English pope?

21. Which British king married May of Teck?

22. At the outbreak of World War I, who was the British Prime Minister?

23. What great structure, designed by Joseph Paxton, was built in 1851?

24. What were the names of the two princes believed to have been murdered in the Tower of London in 1483?

25. What unusual accident eventually caused the death of the Prince of Wales, eldest son of George II?

26. Which of Dickens's novels depicts the struggles and strife of factory workers in Victorian England?

EVERSLEY, THE WHITE HART 1906 57011

CASTLETON, SPEEDWELL CAVERN 1909 61785

27. How old was William Shakespeare when he got married? 24, 25, 19, or 18?

28. What crime occurred on 8 August 1963 that shocked public opinion in Britain?

29. Who had to hide in an oak tree to save his life after a military defeat?

30. After Henry VIII's Dissolution of the Monasteries, what are some of the new owners of the monastery buildings rumoured to have done with some of the illuminated manuscripts they found?

KING'S LYNN, HIGH STREET 1908 60023

31. In July 1888, 1,500 female employees went on strike at a factory at Bow in East London. What did they manufacture?

32. Who was the Irish saint who legend says saw the Loch Ness Monster in Scotland?
St Columba, St Patrick, St Andrew, or St Aidan?

33. Which English woman made this prophecy:
'Carriages without horses shall go, And accidents fill the world with woe. Around the world thoughts shall fly, In the twinkling of an eye.'?

34. Which tax was levied between 1696 and 1851?

35. How long did the Hundred Years' War last? 116 years, 94 years, 100 years, or 108 years?

36. Who was called the 'Old Pretender'?

37. In 1629 William Harvey published the details of a discovery he had made. What was it?

38. Put these wars and battles in the order in which they took place:
A. The Battle of Agincourt
B. The Battle of Hastings
C. Marston Moor
D. Wars of the Roses

39. In British army slang, what was a 'dead man'?

40. When was the Poll Tax first introduced in England?

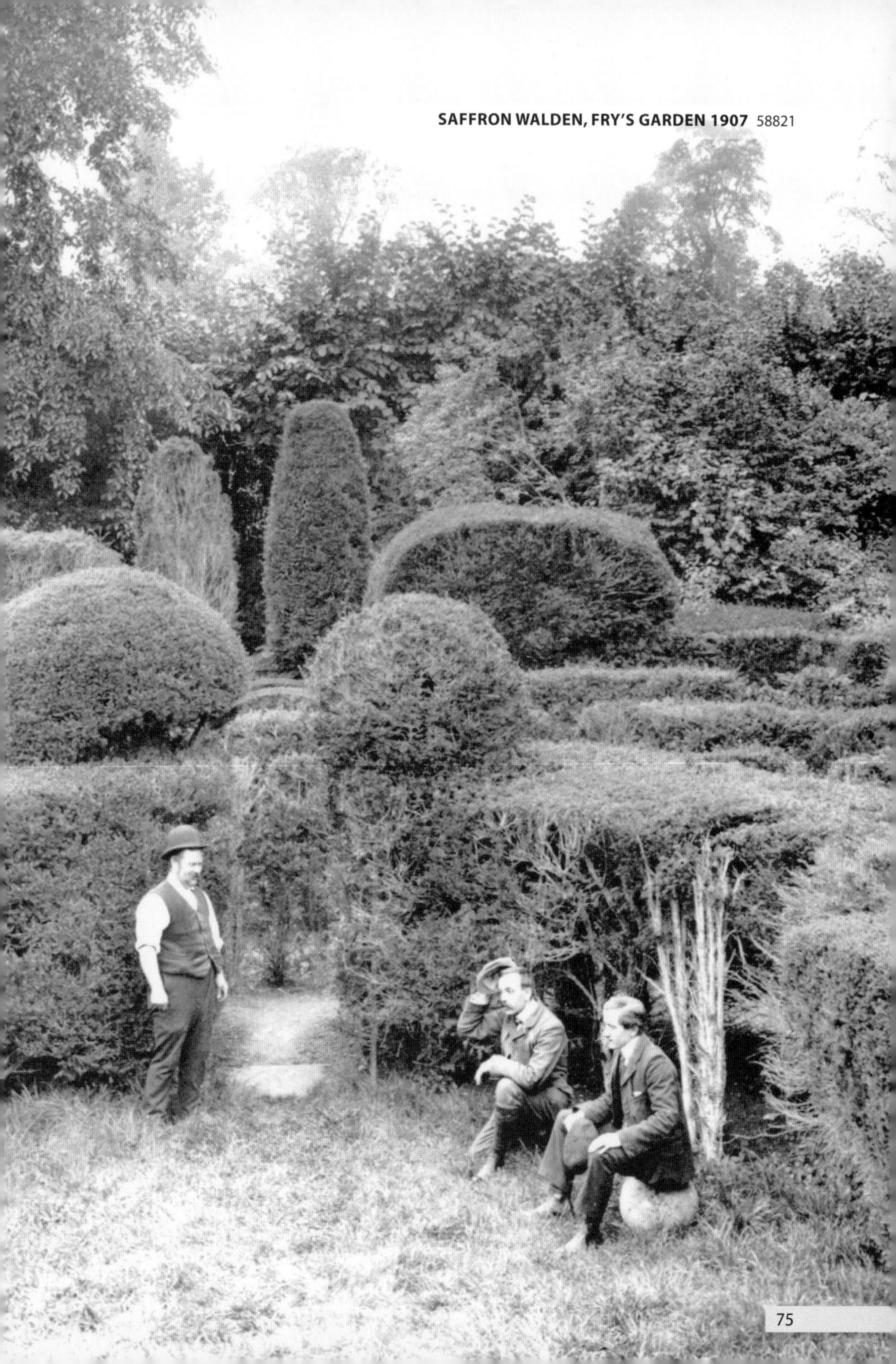

SAFFRON WALDEN, FRY'S GARDEN 1907 58821

CLOVELLY, POST OFFICE, TRANSFER OF MAIL 1936 87551

41. Who was the first Prime Minister of Britain?

42. What is pannage?

43. What were the Welshmen of the Rebecca Riots, who dressed up as women, protesting against?

44. How many people did the 1715 Riot Act have to be read to, in order for them to be guilty of a felony, and liable to the punishment of death? 6, 12, 27, or 250?

CHALFORD, THE VILLAGE 1910 62713

45. What was the joint stock company, the South Sea Company, set up in 1711 to trade in?

46. In the Middle Ages, a split stick was used by royal officials to record sums of money paid. Notches were cut on it representing payments. What was it called?

EASTBOURNE, THE PIER 1925 77946

WEYMOUTH, THE SANDS 1909 61597

47. When did the Union Jack achieve its present pattern?

48. In 1752, September 2 was followed by September 14. What was the name of the new calendar system that involved this adjustment?

NEWBY BRIDGE, THE SWAN HOTEL 1914 67414

49. Coffee houses were patronised by literary giants such as Dryden, Johnson, and Pope. How many coffee houses were there in London in the 18th century?
10, 50, 250, or 1800?

50. Who was the first British Prime Minister to live at 10 Downing Street?

TENBY 1890 28091

GENERAL HISTORY QUIZ ANSWERS

1. Winston Churchill.

2. Opium.

3. Edgehill.

4. Lord Melbourne.

5. Dr Crippen. He buried her body in the basement of his London house.

6. For giving false evidence against Catholics.

7. They murdered people and sold their corpses to unscrupulous surgeons for dissection.

8. German.

9. The Tolpuddle Martyrs.

10. The Battle of Bosworth Field.

11. Lloyd George.

12. Emmeline Pankhurst.

13. 1881.

14. King John.

15. Manchester.

16. Henry VIII and Anne Boleyn.

17. Marie Antoinette.

18. Charles I. The weather was cold and he did not want to be seen shivering.

19. Mary I, the daughter of Henry VIII and Catherine of Aragon. She married Philip II of Spain, and was a devout Catholic. She earned her nickname from her persecution of Protestants.

20. Adrian IV, born Nicholas Brakespeare in 1100.

21. George V (she was known in this country as Mary).

22. Herbert Asquith.

23. The Crystal Palace.

24. Edward V and his brother Richard Duke of York, the sons of Edward IV.

25. He was hit on the head by a cricket ball.

26. 'Hard Times', published in 1854.

27. 18.

28. The Great Train Robbery.

GENERAL HISTORY QUIZ ANSWERS

29. Charles II.

30. They used them as lavatory paper.

31. Matches. They worked at the Bryant and May factory.

32. St Columba, born cAD521.

33. Mother Shipton, born in Norfolk in 1485.

34. Window Tax, which was payable on a house with more than six windows.

35. 116 years, between 1337 and 1453.

36. James III (the son of James II). In 1715 he gathered together a force of 10,000 men and invaded England. The Jacobites fought their way as far as Preston, where they were dispersed.

37. The circulation of the blood. He was physician extraordinary to James I.

38. B (1066) A (1415) D (1455-85) C (1644).

39. An empty bottle.

40. In 1222, on every person over the age of 14.

41. Robert Walpole. As first Lord of the Treasury between 1721 and 1742 he presided over the cabinet.

42. The right of tenants to graze their swine in the woods of a manor.

43. They destroyed turnpike houses, being unhappy about the levels of tolls.

44. 12.

45. Slaves in Latin America.

46. A tally.

47. In 1801, when the cross of St Patrick was added to the crosses of St George and St Andrew.

48. The Gregorian Calendar.

49. 1800.

50. Sir Robert Walpole (1676-1745).

FRANCIS FRITH

PIONEER VICTORIAN PHOTOGRAPHER

Francis Frith, founder of the world-famous photographic archive, was a complex and multi-talented man. A devout Quaker and a highly successful Victorian businessman, he was philosophical by nature and pioneering in outlook. By 1855 he had already established a wholesale grocery business in Liverpool, and sold it for the astonishing sum of £200,000, which is the equivalent today of over £15,000,000. Now in his thirties, and captivated by the new science of photography, Frith set out on a series of pioneering journeys up the Nile and to the Near East.

INTRIGUE AND EXPLORATION

He was the first photographer to venture beyond the sixth cataract of the Nile. Africa was still the mysterious 'Dark Continent', and Stanley and Livingstone's historic meeting was a decade into the future. The conditions for picture taking confound belief. He laboured for hours in his wicker dark-room in the sweltering heat of the desert, while the volatile chemicals fizzed dangerously in their trays. Back in London he exhibited his photographs and was 'rapturously cheered' by members of the Royal Society. His reputation as a photographer was made overnight.

VENTURE OF A LIFE-TIME

By the 1870s the railways had threaded their way across the country, and Bank Holidays and half-day Saturdays had been made obligatory by Act of Parliament. All of a sudden the working man and his family were able to enjoy days out, take holidays, and see a little more of the world.

With typical business acumen, Francis Frith foresaw that these new tourists would enjoy having souvenirs to commemorate their days out. For the next thirty years he travelled the country by train and by pony and trap, producing fine photographs of seaside resorts and beauty spots that were keenly bought by millions of Victorians. These prints were painstakingly pasted into family albums and pored over during the dark nights of winter, rekindling precious memories of summer excursions. Frith's studio was soon supplying retail shops all over the country, and by 1890 F Frith & Co had become the greatest specialist photographic publishing company in the world, with over 2,000 sales outlets, and pioneered the picture postcard.

FRANCIS FRITH'S LEGACY

Francis Frith had died in 1898 at his villa in Cannes, his great project still growing. By 1970 the archive he created contained over a third of a million pictures showing 7,000 British towns and villages.

Frith's legacy to us today is of immense significance and value, for the magnificent archive of evocative photographs he created provides a unique record of change in the cities, towns and villages throughout Britain over a century and more. Frith and his fellow studio photographers revisited locations many times down the years to update their views, compiling for us an enthralling and colourful pageant of British life and character.

We are fortunate that Frith was dedicated to recording the minutiae of everyday life. For it is this sheer wealth of visual data, the painstaking chronicle of changes in dress, transport, street layouts, buildings, housing and landscape that captivates us so much today, offering us a powerful link with the past and with the lives of our ancestors.

Computers have now made it possible for Frith's many thousands of images to be accessed almost instantly. The archive offers every one of us an opportunity to examine the places where we and our families have lived and worked down the years. Its images, depicting our shared past, are now bringing pleasure and enlightenment to millions around the world a century and more after his death.

For further information visit: www.francisfrith.co.uk

FRITH PRODUCTS & SERVICES

Francis Frith would doubtless be pleased to know that the pioneering publishing venture he started in 1860 still continues today. Over a hundred and forty years later, The Francis Frith Collection continues in the same innovative tradition and is now one of the foremost publishers of vintage photographs in the world. Some of the current activities include:

INTERIOR DECORATION

Today Frith's photographs can be seen framed and as giant wall murals in thousands of pubs, restaurants, hotels, banks, retail stores and other public buildings throughout the country. In every case they enhance the unique local atmosphere of the places they depict and provide reminders of gentler days in an increasingly busy and frenetic world.

PRODUCT PROMOTIONS

Frith products are used by many major companies to promote the sales of their own products or to reinforce their own history and heritage. Frith promotions have been used by Hovis bread, Courage beers, Scots Porage Oats, Colman's mustard, Cadbury's foods, Mellow Birds coffee, Dunhill pipe tobacco, Guinness, and Bulmer's Cider.

GENEALOGY AND FAMILY HISTORY

As the interest in family history and roots grows world-wide, more and more people are turning to Frith's photographs of Great Britain for images of the towns, villages and streets where their ancestors lived; and, of course, photographs of the churches and chapels where their ancestors were christened, married and buried are an essential part of every genealogy tree and family album.

FRITH PRODUCTS

All Frith photographs are available Framed or just as Mounted Prints and Posters (size 23 x 16 inches). These may be ordered from the address below. From time to time other products - Address Books, Calendars, Table Mats, etc - are available.

THE INTERNET

Already one hundred thousand Frith photographs can be viewed and purchased on the internet through the Frith websites and a myriad of partner sites.

For more detailed information on Frith companies and products, look at these sites:

www.francisfrith.co.uk

www.francisfrith.com

(for North American Visitors)

See the complete list of Frith Books at:

www.francisfrith.co.uk

This web site is regularly updated with the latest list of publications from The Francis Frith Collection. If you wish to buy books relating to another part of the country that your local bookshop does not stock, you may purchase on-line.

For further information, trade, or author enquiries please contact us at the address below:

The Francis Frith Collection, Frith's Barn, Teffont, Salisbury, Wiltshire, England SP3 5QP.

Tel: +44 (0)1722 716 376 Fax: +44 (0)1722 716 881

e-mail: sales@francisfrith.co.uk

See all Frith products on the internet at www.francisfrith.co.uk